TAKING CHARLIE

by Neil Warhurst

Adapted from the Radio Play in collaboration
with Goofus

SAMUEL FRENCH

samuelfrench.co.uk

For Amateur Production Enquiries

United Kingdom and World
excluding north america
plays@samuelfrench.co.uk
020 7255 4302/01

Each title is subject to availability from Samuel French,
depending upon country of performance.

THINKING ABOUT PERFORMING A SHOW?

There are thousands of plays and musicals available to perform from Samuel French right now, and applying for a licence is easier and more affordable than you might think

---

From classic plays to brand new musicals, from monologues to epic dramas, there are shows for everyone.

Plays and musicals are protected by copyright law so if you want to perform them, the first thing you'll need is a licence. This simple process helps support the playwright by ensuring they get paid for their work, and means that you'll have the documents you need to stage the show in public.

Not all our shows are available to perform all the time, so it's important to check and apply for a licence before you start rehearsals or commit to doing the show.

LEARN MORE & FIND THOUSANDS OF SHOWS

Browse our full range of plays and musicals and find out more about how to license a show

www.samuelfrench.co.uk/perform

Talk to the friendly experts in our Licensing team for advice on choosing a show, and help with licensing

plays@samuelfrench.co.uk   020 7387 9373

Acting Editions

BORN TO PERFORM

Playscripts designed from the ground up to work the way you do in rehearsal, performance and study

---

Larger, clearer text for easier reading

Wider margins for notes

Performance features such as character and props lists, sound and lighting cues, and more

---

+ CHOOSE A SIZE AND STYLE TO SUIT YOU

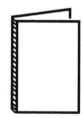

STANDARD EDITION

Our regular paperback book at our regular size

SPIRAL-BOUND EDITION

The same size as the Standard Edition, but with a sturdy, easy-to-fold, easy-to-hold spiral-bound spine

LARGE EDITION

A4 size and spiral bound, with larger text and a blank page for notes opposite every page of text. Perfect for technical and directing use

---

ABOUT THE AUTHOR

Neil is a writer and actor. Two of his theatre plays, *Taking Charlie* and *Dumbheads*, were first broadcast on BBC Radio 4. He's also written and performed (in collaboration with Goofus Artistic Director, Paul Barnhill) numerous radio comedy series. These include *Clayton Grange*, about brilliantly stupid scientists (starring Anthony Head), *Edge Falls* set in a monstrous retail park (starring Sarah Lancashire) and *The Spaceship*, a mock-documentary following life on-board a space-ship (starring James Fleet). Neil adapted his first radio series *Beyond the Pole* into a screenplay, which was released in 2010. This story about two men walking to the North Pole stars Stephen Mangan, Rhys Thomas and Alexander Skarsgard.

AUTHOR'S NOTE

The real events that took place in 1978 are the very loose bones that hold this play together. The rest, the body of it, is completely made up. Now it's up to the actors to bring this corpse to life.

You can be as flexible with the staging as I have been with the truth. A big budget allows you a spectacle; car crashes, dismembered limbs, and panoramic Swiss scenery. You may prefer to simply use a suitcase and a few props. If you have the means to display authentic "silent film" captions on an enormous screen, go for it. Otherwise the actors can hold up some cardboard signs. And it's possible, when Chaplin himself comes to life, you will have found someone able to mimic all the Little Tramp's mannerisms and nuances. More likely whoever's playing Stefan will be doubling up. He could do it authentically, or badly; he could make a joke of his poor interpretation. You could also present Chaplin as a shadow behind a screen, or a puppet on strings. It doesn't matter, because if the actor playing Alek believes he is seeing his hero, the audience will believe it too. Budget, therefore, is not so important. What's crucial is simplicity, so action can move swiftly and seamlessly from one location to another.

Bear in mind also, I created this play in collaboration with a theatre company called Goofus. Their name means "idiot", and they believe that idiocy, in all its forms, is something to celebrate. So find your inner idiot. We all have one. The biggest idiots are those who don't realise they're idiots, like Stefan, or the numerous dictators who try to bestride the globe, or the Trumps of this world, who have no idea how truly hilarious they are.

Alek and Stefan are classic clowns; the double-act between them makes or breaks the show. Bring the audience in on the joke – look at them, talk to them – because in clowning there is no fourth wall. Let them know you're nothing but flawed actors, telling a story in the best way you can. Laugh at yourself.

But at the same time remember, for the characters, the stakes are enormous. There's a lot going on – love, pride, jealousy, humiliation, anger – all this really matters and should be played with passion and absolute truth. It's a delicate balancing act; having fun, but not shying away from the darkness. Chaplin himself was the master of this interplay between light and dark, and in his words...

"To truly laugh, you must be able to take your pain, and play with it".

Neil Warhurst

**Other plays by NEIL WARHURST
published and licensed by Samuel French**

Beyond The Pole

**FIND PERFECT PLAYS TO PERFORM AT
www.samuelfrench.co.uk/perform**

Taking Charlie is adapted from the afternoon play of the same name, broadcast on BBC Radio 4 in 2003 and directed by Peter Kavanagh.

The theatre play was first performed by Goofus at Harrogate Theatre, on the 9 April 2014.

Cast:

Stefan – Paul Barnhill
Alek – Guy Hargreaves
Sylvie – Lindsay Allen
Chaplin – Paul Barnhill
Oona Chaplin – Lindsay Allen

Director – Andy Williams
Production Manager – Hannah Blamire

CHARACTERS

Alec and **Stefan** – unemployed auto-mechanics from Bulgaria

Sylvie – a Swiss seamstress/taxidermist

Chaplin – a resurrected version of the great dead comedian

Oona Chaplin – widow of Charlie

PROLOGUE

A caption card, like that from a silent film, is projected onto a screen:

Caption: Switzerland. Land of Opportunity.

Lights up on a panoramic mountain range, a road sign pointing to "Lausanne 10 kms", and a cardboard cut out of a cow. Two shabby men appear, wearing long-coats, and carrying battered suitcases. STEFAN *is aggressive and charming,* ALEK *is gentle and awkward. They look at the signpost, and the cow, and sit down to wait by the side of the road.*

The cow moos. Birds sing. After a moment, ALEK *addresses the audience.*

ALEK In 1978 two Eastern European, refugee, auto mechanics kidnapped and ransomed the body of Charlie Chaplin... because they wanted money to set up their very own garage. This is a true story. What you are about to see...is not.

We hear loud Swiss folk music.

A cardboard cutout of a Citroën 2CV comes onto the stage. Behind the wheel is a woman, SYLVIE, *dressed in traditional Swiss costume.*

A new caption appears on the screen:

Caption: Opportunity Number One.

Suddenly the car stops, and the music cuts. The engine makes an exploding sound, and a puff of dirty smoke comes out of the bonnet.

The immigrants stand, sensing an opening. **ALEK** *opens a suitcase, and pulls out a toolbox.* **STEFAN** *unbuttons his shirt to reveal a forest of chest hair.*

SYLVIE *looks their way.*

Blackout.

ACT I

Scene One

In a dark back alley, STEFAN *is highly wound up, holding his right hand flat on the ground.* ALEK *is nervously holding an axe.*

Caption: Opportunity Number Two.

STEFAN Is it sharp?

ALEK Yea.

STEFAN Do it hard. I want a clean cut. Right?

ALEK Is this a good idea?

STEFAN 'Course it's a good idea! Go on.

    ALEK *raises the axe high in the air...his hand shakes.*

ALEK Now?

STEFAN Yes. No. Higher than that! Then bring it down really hard. Then piss off.

ALEK Piss off?

STEFAN Don't piss off. Make a noise. Get someone – the police – whatever – then piss off.

ALEK Yea.

    STEFAN *breathes out heavily, psyching himself up.*

What shall I do with it?

STEFAN What?

ALEK The hand?

STEFAN I don't bloody care! Do what you want!

ALEK It's your hand –!

STEFAN What good is this hand to me here?! Eh? Just do it!

ALEK What if they find out?

STEFAN Stop bloody asking questions! They won't find out!

ALEK Sylvie will find out –

STEFAN No she won't.

ALEK She won't like it.

STEFAN She'll like it when I give her a massive cheque. It's a good plan. Foolproof. As long as you do it right.

He shuts his eyes.

STEFAN Go on. Really whack it. Nice and –

ALEK *brings down the axe weakly. It nips the edge of* STEFAN*'s wrist.*

STEFAN *screams silently. Blood starts spurting from the wound.*

You missed!

ALEK I got the edge of it –

STEFAN You need to get all of it! Do it again! Aah! Oh my – take it off. Finish it. Finish it! Do it quick!

ALEK *re-takes position with the axe and brings it down. It is a perfect cut.*

STEFAN *staggers away, blood pumping from his stump.*

ALEK Alright?

STEFAN *falls over.*

ALEK *runs off, shouting for help.*

Scene Two

Mist rises. Bolts slides. Enormous iron gates open.

STEFAN *emerges into the light in a long coat, with a very long prisoner's beard, his right hand hidden deep in his pocket. The gates slam shut behind him.*

ALEK *appears through the mist.*

STEFAN Sylvie?

ALEK Stefan...!

STEFAN *turns away, and shouts.*

STEFAN Sylvie!

ALEK Stefan, it's me.

STEFAN Sylvie!

ALEK Sylvie couldn't make it. I'm here.

STEFAN Two years I've been in there.

ALEK Two years and four days actually. And sixteen hours. *(He holds out his hand)* It's good to see you Stefan.

STEFAN *slowly removes his hand from his pocket.*

There is a large, gruesome hook on the end of it.

They're good they are. Is that what they call a prosthetic limb?

STEFAN It's a hook.

ALEK It's great...new technology...

STEFAN It's almost like having a real hand.

ALEK Well...you can pick things up with it. Hooks are good for that.

STEFAN Like what? What can I pick up with it?

ALEK A bucket.

STEFAN A bucket?

ALEK Or...a tin of paint. You could hook right under it. What else?

STEFAN Other hooks.

ALEK Yea and you could hang coats on it.

STEFAN What am I? A coat hook?

ALEK No...I'm just saying it's more adaptable than you –

STEFAN Can I change a spark plug? Can I fix a carburettor? I can't believe you cut it off.

ALEK You told me to! It'd make a fortune you said!

STEFAN Well, it didn't work did it! I'm still broke and now I haven't even got a hand!

Beat.

ALEK Got the other hand.

STEFAN Shut up.

Silence.

She never visited me. Not once.

ALEK I think she was a bit miffed...what with the insurance thing...and the being in prison...and the not having a hand.

STEFAN She could've written.

ALEK You could've written –

STEFAN I can't write, can I! I can take someone's eye out, though –!

STEFAN *suddenly walks off.*

ALEK Stefan –!

STEFAN Stay away from me! I should've left you on the street!

ALEK Do you want a beer?

STEFAN You got beer?

ALEK Yea. Back at the garage.

STEFAN What garage?

ALEK I've got my own garage.

STEFAN You've got your own garage?

ALEK Yea. Come.

    STEFAN *follows, stunned, into –*

Scene Three

There is an old mattress on the floor with a teddy bear on it. There are tools, an old radio, some tins, and the odd tyre.

ALEK It's a place to work...to sleep...to dream.

STEFAN You fixed any cars?

ALEK No.

STEFAN It's not really a garage then, is it.

ALEK produces beer.

ALEK Next week the landlord is bringing in his Citroën CX. I'm fixing it in lieu of rent.

STEFAN In what?

ALEK In lieu of rent.

STEFAN tries repeatedly to open a bottle with his hook hand.

After a while he gives up, angrily grabbing the bottle with his left hand, shoving it down his trousers, and prising the lid off with his arse.

He takes a greedy swig.

STEFAN Shall I open yours?

ALEK No – no. I'll use this.

ALEK produces a bottle opener.

They both drink.

STEFAN Two years with four hundred men. I worked it out... that's eight hundred testicles. I'd stand in the food hall, all those eight hundred balls just hanging there. Swishing. It plays with the mind.

His words hang in the air.

STEFAN You owe me.

ALEK I know.

STEFAN I never said it was you cut it off. I kept quiet.

ALEK If there's anything I can do Stefan...anything. All this...
it's all yours. Ours.

> **STEFAN** *grabs* **ALEK**'s *bottle of beer and drinks, savouring
> every mouthful.*

STEFAN Beer. Oh, that's good. That's what I need. Beer...and
sex. Or sex and beer. Or beer, beer and sex. Or sex, sex, sex
and beer, beer, sex, then another beer, beer, sex, sex...maybe
some cashew nuts, then another beer...

ALEK I haven't stopped dreaming you know...

STEFAN Don't –

ALEK This is just the start –

STEFAN Look at me. Look at me! There is no garage!

ALEK Don't say that. You just have to get back into the swing
of things.

STEFAN Go on, then. Fill me in. What's happening in the world?
What have I missed?

ALEK Um...well...you know that man in the bread shop with
the funny voice and the squint? I can't remember his name.

STEFAN Nor can I.

ALEK He died. That was sad.

STEFAN Right.

ALEK Mr Hauptmann lost a couple of cows. They died. *(Beat)*
You remember that cat? Sylvie used to give it milk. It fell
off a roof.

STEFAN Died.

ALEK   No, very, very badly injured. Leg all floppy. Some boys rescued him. Turned it into a firework. Then he died.

STEFAN *gets up.*

STEFAN   Bloody hell, I think I might go back in –

ALEK   And the worst, saddest thing of all... Charlie Chaplin!

STEFAN   What about him?

ALEK   He died.

STEFAN   Oh for –

ALEK   I loved Charlie Chaplin. Mum and Dad always used to take –

STEFAN *walks decisively away.*

Where are you going?

STEFAN   To see Sylvie. See she's OK.

ALEK   Why, was she a fan?

STEFAN   No! I'm just going to see if she's okay! I want life! I want my wife! Living and breathing...in my arms –

ALEK   Stefan –

STEFAN   I want my seed...exploding!

ALEK   She doesn't want to see you.

STEFAN   What?

ALEK   She told me. She doesn't want to see you.

Beat.

STEFAN   You been seeing a lot of her, have you?

ALEK   You asked me to look out for her. While you were inside. I go round for tea. Sometimes we have fondue.

STEFAN   Right. So why doesn't she want to see me?

ALEK   She thinks you're an arse. She gave me a note...

ALEK *pulls out an envelope, and hands it to* STEFAN.

STEFAN *opens it and reads.*

STEFAN　"You're an arse."

He frowns. He turns the page over. That's it.

There is a lot she is not saying here.

ALEK　She thinks you're an arse.

STEFAN　Yeah, you need to read between the lines.

ALEK　Shall I come with you?

STEFAN　No! And stay away from Sylvie!

STEFAN *runs out of the lock-up.*

Scene Four

SYLVIE sits in a simple bedsit, wearing a plain dress. She sews with needle and thread, and sings a mournful tune.

STEFAN appears outside, clasping a plastic bag.

STEFAN Sylvie? Sylvie!

SYLVIE Who is it?

STEFAN It's me. I'm out.

SYLVIE I don't know who you are.

STEFAN It's your husband. I'm out. *(Beat)* What do you want me to do?

SYLVIE Go back in.

STEFAN rummages in his plastic bag and produces various items.

STEFAN I bring gifts. I bring...carrots. A rabbit. Some rocks. I am a simple man. All I have...comes from the road, the fields, or the generosity of others. But they are gifts from my heart...so they are precious like gold. Soup. I have soup.

SYLVIE What do you want, Stefan?

STEFAN I have missed you. Like a leaf blown from its tree. Without the sap from the tree... I wilt. I want to drink... your sap.

SYLVIE Do you know what I want?

STEFAN Tell me and it is yours.

SYLVIE A divorce.

STEFAN I bring...what else? Another carrot...it looks a little bit like Christ. It is a miracle. We could charge for viewings of the Christ Carrot. We would have pilgrims from around the world –

SYLVIE Did you get my letter?

STEFAN I didn't really understand it.

SYLVIE What is there not to understand? You lied to me.

STEFAN I didn't think you'd go along with it unless I lied. It would've paid all the debts –

SYLVIE Well, it didn't pay the debts, did it? And now you haven't got a hand! We had such dreams, Stefan, but all the time you have this little plan in your head –

STEFAN It was a good plan.

SYLIVE It's stealing! From the country that took you in.

STEFAN They can afford it.

SYLVIE This is exactly what Papa warned me about. You humiliated me.

STEFAN Oh, and bankers do not steal?

SYLVIE He was right all along. The man I married was a liar, a crook, and a cheat!

STEFAN I may be all those things but I am not an arse.

    STEFAN *begins warbling a traditional Bulgarian folk song.*

SYLVIE Don't. I do not need you. I'm doing very nicely on my own.

STEFAN You back wearing the little dress? Doing the little dance?

SYLVIE No. I am sewing.

STEFAN Sewing?

SYLVIE That school taught me something at least. There is a man who throws work my way.

STEFAN What man?

SYLVIE The finest in Lausanne.

STEFAN The finest man?

SYLVIE Taxidermist.

STEFAN You sew dead things?

For the first time we see what she's been sewing: a small stuffed squirrel.

SYLVIE There are so many creatures who need holes to be mended, mounts to be repaired. There are worse jobs. I'm working with animals. You see? Things are taking off for me. I'm paying my own way. I've settled the debts. And I'm happy. So give me one good reason I should take you back?

STEFAN Sylv...all those long two years inside I didn't shave once.

She opens the door a little, breathless.

SYLVIE Oh...

STEFAN Go on. Run your hands through it...

SYLVIE Uh...lift your shirt up.

STEFAN *reveals huge amounts of chest hair.*

STEFAN There's more yet my little busy bee. Look down there... Like the forests of Starazagora –

SYLVIE No... No! You think you're a charmer Stefan Debelyanov, but I'm not falling for you again. Leave me alone!

She slams the door.

STEFAN Sylvie! *(Shouting)* Sylvie! Ok... I understand. You're just like the rest of them. You keep us out in the cold! Well I tell you...you watch out...because the Bulgarians are coming!

SYLVIE Oh, Stefan...

STEFAN *(yelling)* You're all bastards...with your fancy yachts and skiing festivals and your cheesy fondue and little fancy chocolates...and your clocks...and little Heidi with her goats and bells, tinkling...

He fades away in the dark.

Blackout.

ACT II

Scene One

In the lock-up, ALEK *is fixing the Citroën CX, to loud seventies disco music.*

With a series of dextrous movements he manipulates various tools that he pulls from various pockets. ALEK *moves in harmony with the music, like a conjurer, or a cocktail mixer. He knows exactly what he is doing – neat, immaculate, and more confident than we've ever seen him.*

STEFAN *appears in the shadows, watching.*

ALEK *finishes off the performance with a neat little kick. The music cuts and the engine bursts into life. He modestly puts his tools away in his pockets.*

STEFAN *walks into the light.*

STEFAN Not bad. They should call you Frankenstein.

ALEK Frankenstein? *(He laughs nervously)* Why?

STEFAN Because you bring cars back from the dead.

ALEK You can be Igor. Igor. Remember...? He walks like this... *(He does an impression, and the voice)* Igor, Igor...! And he's so ugly, and does whatever he's told...master, master... I'll be Igor.

STEFAN *lies on the mattress.*

STEFAN Mind if I kip here for a few days?

ALEK This is your home.

STEFAN I don't want to live here forever. I just thought we could catch up, have a few beers...

ALEK I haven't got any beer. I have beans. Not many. Seven. But you can have them.

STEFAN It is OK this place. Is it secure?

ALEK Erm...it has a lock. It is a lock-up.

ALEK grabs a bundle of cloth and unwraps it.

I made you a present.

Inside is a large spanner attachment. STEFAN unscrews his hook attachment, and screws on the spanner.

You have a spanner hand.

STEFAN I'm a bloody bionic man! Who says I cannot be a mechanic, eh?

STEFAN goes to the CX, tweaks something, and the engine dies.

ALEK I can make others. Pliers. Oil can. Maybe a drill. Oh – and I got this for Sylvie.

He produces an old sewing machine.

It was dumped. I had to fix the motor, but it's –

STEFAN How are the neighbours? Do they fuss?

ALEK About what?

STEFAN Noise.

ALEK No. The walls are thick.

STEFAN Good. You see... I've been thinking. And I'm thinking... we will have our garage.

ALEK Stefan!

STEFAN With your talents and my brain for business, we'll be unstoppable. But to have a garage...we need investment.

ALEK Have you got an idea?

STEFAN I'm buzzing mate, I'm on fire.

ALEK What's the idea?

STEFAN It's brilliant.

ALEK They're always brilliant.

STEFAN But I can't do this on my own. Are you in?

ALEK I'm in. What is it?

STEFAN We kidnap someone!

Silence.

What? You don't like it?

ALEK I like it, it's brilliant. Really good. Just...

STEFAN What?

ALEK It sounds a lot of trouble.

STEFAN Ply them with vodka, they'll be like pussy cats. Everyone's at it these days. In Italy, behind every fridge in every trattoria, there's some rich bastard trussed up.

Silence.

You owe me. You were nothing. I gave you a dream. My dream of a garage.

ALEK We have a garage –

STEFAN This is a nightmare of a garage. Are you going to piss on my dreams?

ALEK I'd never piss on your dreams.

STEFAN Good. Right. Because you're wasting your talents. You should be doing Mercs, BMWs. Huh? Your father would be so proud. No shitty Moskvitch rust buckets for you, eh?

All we have to do...is think of someone really rich who lives round here.

ALEK Everyone's rich round here.

STEFAN I mean really rich. Riches we couldn't even dream of.

ALEK My landlord?

STEFAN Think big. In fact, let's think famous. Rich and famous!

ALEK I can't think of anyone!

STEFAN Come on.

ALEK There's Charlie Chaplin but he's –

STEFAN Brilliant! We kidnap Chaplin!

ALEK But he's dead.

STEFAN What?

ALEK He died at Christmas. I told you.

STEFAN Did you?

ALEK Yea. We went to visit the grave, actually.

STEFAN Who?

ALEK Me and Sylvie.

STEFAN You know how to treat a lady.

ALEK We had sandwiches. There's no headstone yet, but it's a lovely spot down by the lake. Sad though.

STEFAN It's brilliant!

ALEK No, it's not.

STEFAN We'll have to do it quick.

ALEK What?

STEFAN Nick the body. Then ransom it for shed-loads.

Beat.

ALEK Shouldn't we think it through a bit.

STEFAN Alright. *(He thinks)* It's still brilliant. He's not going to be any trouble, is he, if he's dead. All we've got to do is work out how to get the body from there...to here.

ALEK Here?!

STEFAN How long before you can get this CX up and running?

ALEK *gives the car a little kick. The engine springs to life.*

You see? Genius –

Scene Two

A caption reads: "Opportunity Number Three"

We see a simple dumb show, or a shadow play behind the screen.

ALEK *and* **STEFAN** *rub mud on their faces. They put balaclavas over their heads.* **STEFAN** *screws a spade attachment onto his arm.*

They drive the Citroën CX through the dead of night.

They dig in a graveyard. They pull out, with great difficulty, a very large, very heavy coffin, and stagger off with it.

Scene Three

ALEK *and* STEFAN *lug the coffin into the centre of the lock-up.*

They lower it down.

They sit down to recover, exhausted, and covered in mud.

STEFAN Quality wood, that. Spend that much on a coffin, think what they'll spend to get him back.

ALEK I can't believe that's Charlie Chaplin.

An uneasy silence falls, the coffin impossible to ignore.

STEFAN *turns on the radio.*

NEWSRDR – of Charles Chaplin has been stolen from his grave in Switzerland. The resting place of the great comedian was desecrated under the cover of darkness. A police spokesman said: "The grave is empty, the coffin is gone". The news has shocked the world.

STEFAN Oh, this is big!

NEWSRDR As yet, the identity of the robbers is unknown, but reports suggest the coffin was a heavy oak, and police suspect it took three or more men to lift it.

STEFAN Three or more men...?

NEWSRDR In Geneva today, at the world economic forum, banking heads are meeting to –

STEFAN *delightedly turns down the radio.*

STEFAN They know nothing! Two or three men? I don't think so! Just raw Bulgarian muscle!

ALEK Yea.

STEFAN My family were weightlifters. Champions. My father... he was a weightlifter. My grandfather...he was a weightlifter.

My great-grandfather...he was a weightlifter. My great-grandmother...she was a weightlifter. I wasn't a weightlifter. But I had brains. So I got out. Got to Plovdiv. And now look at me? Eh?

Again, an uneasy silence falls.

ALEK Tell me about the garage, Stefan. How we'll have pits for fixing the cars, and we won't be lying on the floor any more, and there'll be pumps so shiny. Tell it, Stefan.

STEFAN I think you know it, Alek. Tell it yourself –

ALEK It's better when you tell it. How many pits will we have?

STEFAN We'll have two pits. One each. Deep enough to stand in. It'll be on the main road out of Geneva, and there'll be BMWs and Mercs coming in, Lamborghinis –

ALEK And will we have a uniform?

STEFAN Matching. And we'll get a reputation. Only the finest clientele will come to us and we'll screw them for every penny they've got.

ALEK And will we have a kettle for tea breaks?

STEFAN Yea...you're not that ambitious really are you? We'll have it all, Alek.

ALEK Calendars?

STEFAN Calendars, yea. Me and you, Alek. Me and you.

He embraces **ALEK**, *and then starts putting on his coat.*

ALEK Where are you going?

STEFAN Don't let anyone in. Don't fix any more cars. This is your job now.

ALEK My job.

STEFAN Don't mess it up.

ALEK You leaving me alone with –?

STEFAN Hey, he's your hero.

> STEFAN *runs off, then comes back in. He grabs the sewing machine.*

And stay away from Sylvie. Understand?

> STEFAN *runs off.*

Scene Four

SYLVIE *is sewing the eyes on a stuffed animal.*

Other dead creatures surround her, waiting to be mended. The atmosphere makes her uneasy. She sings weakly.

STEFAN *arrives outside clutching the sewing machine.*

STEFAN Sylvie! Sylvie! See what I bring you. I bring you –

He puts the sewing machine down, hiding it.

– I bring you nothing! No gifts. Just myself. A simple, humble, sorry, peasant. The one thing I bring...is a new dawn! Take it, or leave it.

SYLVIE I'll leave it.

STEFAN This time it is a different new dawn. This time I have...a job.

SYLVIE What job?

STEFAN A good job. You will never have to work again.

SYLVIE I want to work.

STEFAN And so you shall. But not...this work. These animals. They do not make you happy. You can tell that taxidermist to go stuff himself.

STEFAN *laughs at his own joke.* **SYLVIE** *doesn't.*

Sylvie?

SYLVIE What job?

STEFAN It is on the main road out of Geneva. On the pump. Big petrol station. Pumping. A man could not have a more honest job.

SYLVIE *opens the door.*

SYLVIE I want to trust you, Stefan.

STEFAN You can trust me. Every day I get the train. I work. I come back. I will work, I will save...and one day we will be so rich –

SYLVIE I do not need to be rich.

STEFAN Nor do I. Comfortable. That is all I want. All I want is to keep you warm.

STEFAN *embraces her in his big coat.*

In the darkness, ALEK *appears, watching.*

SYLVIE I've had enough of dead things.

STEFAN No more dead things. Life. Oh – I did bring you one gift.

STEFAN *picks up the sewing machine and gives it to her. She takes it, stunned.*

It took some mending.

SYLVIE You remembered!

STEFAN What?

SYLVIE You remembered.

STEFAN Yep.

They kiss.

SYLVIE Is that really two years growth?

STEFAN It is, little lady.

SYLVIE *jumps on* STEFAN. *They back into the door, shutting it.* ALEK *looks on.*

SYLVIE Oh, I've missed your smell...the smell of the earth and... mud? You big Eastern European! Like you've been digging potatoes...

They laugh, then SYLVIE *yelps.*

Use your other hand...!

STEFAN Sorry.

Scene Five

At the phone box in the town square, STEFAN *takes a few coins from* ALEK.

ALEK How's Sylvie?

STEFAN Oh, she's good. Very good. Very, very good. *(He puts coins in the slot and starts dialing)* How's Charlie?

ALEK Good. Quiet.

STEFAN Like I said...no trouble. *(He waits)* And I am not so much of an arse, eh?

STEFAN *yells aggressively.*

Is this the Chaplin house?

Right! We're kidnappers! We've got Charlie – if you want him back – hello? Hello?

Well, could you get her?

When is she back?

Right, OK – who are you?

Monica? *(To* ALEK*)* It's Monica the maid.

Can you take a message?

Great. OK. *(Aggressive again)* We're kidnappers. We've got Charlie Chaplin – what?

Alright, well get another pen. *(To* ALEK*)* She's just getting a pen that works.

Yea, a red pen is fine. More menacing. Yea, and put it in capitals. OK – we're kidnappers. We've got Charlie. If you want him back we want six hundred thousand Swiss francs. We'll give you till Tuesday...right? – that's Tuesday week. Not this Tuesday... 'Cos that doesn't give you – what with Sunday and the bank holiday...so that's Tuesday the...the... what date is it today? Right. *(Counting quickly)* Third, fourth, fifth, sixth... erm – the twelfth! We want it on the twelfth! Put it in your diary!

STEFAN *hangs up. They exchange a high five.*

Blackout.

ACT III

Scene One

STEFAN *and* ALEK *meet again at the phone box.*

Time has passed; STEFAN *is now smarter, and beardless.*

He puts money in the slot.

STEFAN Hello? Is that Monica? *(Menacing)* Right, we –
I'm fine. How are you?
Good. We need the –
No, we have body.
No, we have body.
We have body.
Listen, you don't seem to understand, you tell Mrs Chaplin
that we want six hundred –
We are not cranks!

She hangs up. He puts down the phone astonished.

Cranks...?

ALEK I like the...er...the new chin.

STEFAN It's not a new chin. I've had a shave. It's for my new job.

ALEK You've got a new job?

STEFAN No. This is my new job. What we're doing. This is so
Sylvie thinks I have a job.

ALEK Did you tell her about Charlie?

STEFAN Of course not! She wouldn't understand what I'm doing.

ALEK What does she think you're doing?

STEFAN Pump attendant.

ALEK That is a good job.

STEFAN No. This is a good job, what we're doing –

ALEK But they don't believe we have the body –

STEFAN They will! It's a good plan. It's just a matter of time.

Scene Two

In the bedsit, **STEFAN** *sits by a radio, fuming quietly, as* **SYLVIE** *waits in bed.*

RADIO The disappearance of Charlie Chaplin's body continues to baffle police. One theory is that fanatical fans have taken him to England, keen to bury him in the land of his birth. Others believe the robbery to be anti-Semitic, in protest at his presence in a Christian cemetery. Police are also investigating claims that neo nazis disinterred the comedy genius in revenge for his film *The Great Dictator.* They dismissed as ridiculous claims that the body is being ransomed –

STEFAN *irritably snaps off the radio.*

SYLVIE Are you coming to bed?

STEFAN *gets into bed.*

To think there are people who would do such a thing. Cuddle me.

STEFAN *puts his arm around her neck, the hook hanging in front of her face.*

Stefan, can you make a new attachment? Something padded you can wear in bed. Something soft and nice.

STEFAN Yes, yes.

SYLVIE Alek took me there, you know.

STEFAN Where?

SYLVIE Chaplin's grave. We had a picnic.

STEFAN Oh, yes, he told me.

SYLVIE He loved Charlie Chaplin –

STEFAN I know.

SYLVIE So did his mama and papa –

STEFAN I know all this!

SYLVIE And has he told you what happened to them –

STEFAN Yes!

SYLVIE Why are you so angry?

STEFAN I'm not angry. Only because of what they did to his mama and papa.

SYLVIE It was just a little strike.

STEFAN That is communism for you. We were animals in cages. Why do you think we came here?

SYLVIE How is Alek?

STEFAN Very busy now. Fixing many, many cars. Too busy for fondue.

SYLVIE Good. I'm glad. Everything is working out. For both of you.

STEFAN Yes. Yes. So...can you lend me a little money?

SYLVIE I'm sorry?

STEFAN Have you got any...?

SYLVIE You need some –

STEFAN Just a little.

SYLVIE But you are working –

STEFAN It is my first month. I do not get paid until the end.

SYLVIE *hesitates.*

Unless, maybe you think we should talk to Papa.

SYLVIE Why would I do that?

STEFAN Well...he's family.

SYLIVE No, he's not. He didn't even come to our wedding.

STEFAN Time...it heals.

SYLVIE You are still immigrant scum. If you're not good enough for him, I'm not good enough for him.

STEFAN Life is a lot easier...with a banker in the family.

SYLVIE We do not need his dirty money.

STEFAN No?

SYLVIE No.

She reaches under her bed, and pulls out a money box.

I never have stopped dreaming. I've been saving a little each week. The little shop on the high street. Tell it, Stefan.

STEFAN You know it, Sylvie.

SYLVIE It's better when you tell it.

STEFAN You are talking about the flower shop?

SYLVIE No, not that one.

STEFAN The dry cleaners?

SYLVIE No.

STEFAN The shop selling the little cake decorations?

SYLVIE No! The haberdashery!

STEFAN Ah, yes.

SYLVIE Don't you remember? Isn't that why you got me the sewing machine?

STEFAN Of course it is.

SYLVIE A good, honest business, serving ordinary people. And how much money will we make?

STEFAN Just enough to get by.

SYLIVE We won't be greedy. Enough to pay rent on our little cottage, with a little garden. And we can grow our own vegetables. Carrots and broccoli and courgette...tell it, Stefan.

STEFAN Cabbage.

SYLVIE Cabbage. Turnips. And what else will we grow?

STEFAN Er...sprouts?

SYLVIE No. Something much more important than that.

STEFAN Peas?

STLVIE No, we will grow...a baby. Two babies! A family. Imagine that.

STEFAN So how about the money?

SYLVIE You need it now?

STEFAN If you have it. Then I can relax and make babies and all that stuff.

She takes out a large wad of notes, and hands one to him.

SYLVIE And when you get paid, you will save with me?

STEFAN Of course.

He gestures that two notes might be useful. She gives him two notes.

Thank you. I will see you tomorrow.

SYLVIE What about –?

STEFAN Tomorrow.

He runs off, giving a thumbs up as he goes.

Scene Four

ALEK *is finishing a "pair of pliers" hand attachment.*

He talks to the coffin behind him.

ALEK   Can I just say... I love your stuff. I'm a big fan. Well, I was only small, but I remember you, with your funny walk, swinging your cane, fighting the baddies. That bit where you're watching the blind flower girl because she's so beautiful, but she doesn't know you're there, and empties a bucket of water in your face, I killed myself laughing at that – sorry Charlie, I bet you get this all the time, fans going on.

ALEK *gets back to his work for a moment.*

And that bit in the factory, where you accidentally knock your boss into the machine. And he goes through the wheels and cogs and he gets stuck inside, and at lunchtime you feed him his soup through a chicken. Classic. Sorry.

ALEK *works for a second.*

It's just they were special times...the cinema in Plovdiv, Mum and Dad, me...

A flick of light, the click-click of a projector, light flickers on his face. Mum and Dad appear, put a child's outfit round his neck, and sit either side of him as though watching a film.

...we always sat in row G. At the end, in case I needed the toilet. You up there on the big screen, Mum and Dad laughing – Dad with enormous teeth like a beaver... *(Dad shows his enormous front teeth)* ...Mum with a laugh that could kill a man. *(Mum laughs like a drain)* Yea, we were poor, yea we were oppressed slaves of a totalitarian dictatorship, but those moments with you we were happy, and all I remember is the laughing and laughing and laughing...

A pain rises within and a silent scream comes from his mouth. Mum and Dad fade away into the darkness, and the child's outfit falls to the floor.

(*agonised, OTT*)... And then they died! They died...both of them! Arrested! Shot! Blasted in the head! Two innocents slaughtered!

He pulls himself together, and the pain subsides.

Sorry, I'm going on again.

He goes back to his work.

I got more into horror, after that. Do you like horror films, Charlie? Have you seen *Dawn of the Dead*?

STEFAN *enters the lock-up.*

STEFAN They're talking bollocks on the radio.

ALEK (*mishearing*) Oh. Are there? That's weird.

STEFAN *stares at him.*

STEFAN They are talking bollocks. Not there are talking bollocks. We must show them we are not cranks.

He sees the pliers attachment, grabs it, and screws it on.

Perfect. Help me get the lid open. Can you make this into an attachment? (*He grabs the teddy bear*) Sylvie wants something soft in bed. You know...

ALEK That's my teddy.

STEFAN Sylvie's.

ALEK Mum and Dad gave me that before –

STEFAN Sylvie's now. You want Sylvie to be happy in bed?

ALEK Yes.

STEFAN *starts trying to pull out the nails on the coffin.*

Stefan? You can't do that!

STEFAN Get the wrench! You want to eat in the next six months?
Help me.

*ALEK approaches with the wrench and starts levering
up the lid.*

ALEK They wouldn't like me doing this.

STEFAN Who?

ALEK Mum and Dad.

STEFAN It's a body. Like any other.

ALEK It's Charlie Chaplin.

STEFAN He's dead now. And so are they. What makes him so
special?

*Together they gingerly shift the lid over. They gasp, and
reel.*

Not so funny now, eh Charlie?

STEFAN *takes a Polaroid camera out of his pocket.*

ALEK What's that for?

STEFAN *goes in for a shot.*

STEFAN Cranks?! Come on Charlie. Smile!

He takes a photo, and the paper slides out.

ALEK He's still got it, hasn't he...

Scene Five

STEFAN *and* ALEK *are in the phone box.*

On the other side of the stage, a phone is ringing on a table.

OONA CHAPLIN *appears, dressed in black. She picks up the phone, and speaks in a cool, high society New York accent.*

OONA Hello...hello?

STEFAN It's me.

OONA Who?

STEFAN I'm not stupid am I? I'm not going to tell you who I am.

OONA Oh...is that the *(slightly mocking)* kidnapper?

STEFAN So you believe us now, eh?

OONA I believe you have possession of my husband's corpse, yes.

Beat.

STEFAN Who is this?

OONA Oona Chaplin. Charlie's widow.

STEFAN Great. Straight to the horse's mouth. Here's the deal, we want six hundred thousand Swiss francs. If you want to see your husband again you'll get the money by –

OONA I won't be seeing my husband again. Not in this world anyhow...

STEFAN No, but if you want him back, get the money, or else!

OONA Or else what?

Beat.

STEFAN Or else you won't get him back.

OONA I can't have him back. He's dead. Nothing you or I can do will change that.

STEFAN We're not messing about here, Mrs C. I know they're tapping the phone and you want me gabbing as long as possible just in case I slip up which I won't but I'll make this brief anyway...if you want your beloved back resting in peace, you get that money by Friday.

OONA No, allow me to be brief – I'm a grieving woman, and you taking Charlie makes it all a little harder, but Charlie's gone now. His soul has left his body. My husband is in heaven and in my heart-

STEFAN I thought you were being brief –

OONA Briefly, then, I'm not giving you one cent.

Beat.

STEFAN You're bluffing.

OONA No. You can't harm Charlie now. I can remember how he was. If I really need to see him, I can watch a movie. So briefly, Mr Kidnapper, in reference to your money, you can damn well whistle for it!

She hangs the phone up.

STEFAN *stares at the phone, frozen.*

ALEK What did she say?

STEFAN She...she said she doesn't want him back.

They look at each other.

Blackout.

ACT IV

Scene One

In the lock-up ALEK *works away at a piece of metal, as* STEFAN *paces furiously.*

After a moment...

ALEK I can't believe she doesn't want you, Charlie. Don't worry, stay here as long as you want. I know what it's like, not to be wanted. I was in an orphanage –

STEFAN What are you doing?

ALEK Telling him about the –

STEFAN He doesn't want to know about the orphanage.

ALEK He might. He was in an orphanage. So...no one wanted me for years, Charlie. I had no one, and nothing...except teddy.

He picks up the teddy bear, and starts screwing the metal into its bottom.

And Dad's old toolbox. That kept me going. I was going to be as good as him. Fix anything. Mend anything. Make anything –

STEFAN He's dead! Will you shut it!

ALEK Sorry.

STEFAN I need to think! One of us has to.

Silence.

ALEK Perhaps have a –

STEFAN Ssh.

ALEK – have a dump?

STEFAN What?

ALEK You have good ideas there, don't you.

STEFAN I do. Yea, I'll have a dump.

ALEK That usually helps.

STEFAN Yea.

STEFAN *disappears in the back.*

ALEK I'm sorry, Charlie. He doesn't mean it. I don't know where I'd be without Stefan. I wouldn't be here, that's for sure. I'd still be in Plovdiv. No friends. No home. That's where we met. On the street. He had nothing either. Except one thing...his dream.

We begin to hear Swiss folk music.

He gave me his dream, Charlie.

On the screen we see images of picture book Switzerland: mountains and lakes, skiing, and alpine horns.

Against this background, a dance routine begins: STEFAN *in a Swiss hat and coat,* SYLVIE *in traditional Swiss dress.* ALEK *joins in with his tools.*

A dream of freedom, not fear, in a place of light, not dark.

On the screen behind we see images of wealth: yachts, bankers, and money.

A place bound by togetherness, where you can be what you want to be, a new life in a land of opportunity –

The dance comes to a climax with STEFAN's *trousers around his ankles. He begins to yell –*

STEFAN I've got it! I've got it! That's it!

SYLVIE *exits.* **STEFAN** *pulls up his trousers, and begins searching for something.*

ALEK Do you have an idea?

STEFAN A brilliant idea. Oh yes!

> **STEFAN** *finds the axe. He raises it triumphantly, and waggles the fingers on his hand.*

ALEK No! Not the other hand!

STEFAN Not mine! His. A few fingers in an envelope? A little present from the postman with their cornflakes?

He strides to the coffin, pulls aside the coffin lid, and pulls out an arm.

Let's remind her what she's missing. Take it.

ALEK We can't –

STEFAN I'll hold it still, you take off the finger.

ALEK Stefan –

STEFAN Do it!

> **ALEK** *gingerly takes the axe.*

He takes the axe to the finger.

Scene Two

OONA *holds an envelope gingerly in one hand, the phone in the other.*

In the phone box STEFAN *yells confidently.*

STEFAN Yea! And there's plenty more where that came from! You're gonna get him back...bit by bit...until you give us six hundred thousand –

OONA As I said before, you can't harm Charlie –

STEFAN His foot's next, then his arms – you want his head in a box?

OONA If you must –

STEFAN You want him back in bits?

OONA Well, at least we'll have him back.

STEFAN *is stumped.*

Music.

STEFAN *and* ALEK *saw off various parts of Chaplin's corpse, body parts wing their way through the air.* STEFAN *becomes more and more furious until –*

– the music cuts.

STEFAN *yells into the phone.*

STEFAN *(yelling)* Four hundred thousand francs, or we –

OONA *(calmly)* Have you ever heard of Buddhism, Mr Kidnapper?

STEFAN What?

OONA In Tibet, they believe that when a person dies, the soul leaves the body...and the body becomes worthless. In fact they chop up the bodies of their loved ones, and feed them to the eagles...

STEFAN Are you saying Charlie was a Buddhist.

OONA No. I'm just suggesting that we can all take inspiration from the peace-loving peoples of Tibet.

STEFAN *(lost for words)* Peoples of Tibet?

OONA Charlie is gone. His spirit lives. Do what you will with the body.

> **STEFAN** *hands the phone to* **ALEK**.

STEFAN I can't talk to her. It's all Buddha bollocks.

> **ALEK** *takes the phone.*

ALEK Hello? Hello?

OONA Hello?

ALEK Oh wow – I can't believe I'm talking to his wife.

STEFAN Threaten her.

ALEK Can you tell me, of all the films he did, which was his favourite?

STEFAN Tell her we'll cut his bollocks off.

> **STEFAN** *grabs the phone.*

Listen, we'll cut his bollocks off, unless you –

OONA Well, he has no use of them any more, so –

STEFAN Yea, but...that's really humiliating for him. Charlie Chaplin losing his bollocks.

OONA I believe it would perhaps be more humiliating for you to play with another man's balls.

ALEK What's she saying?

Silence.

STEFAN Right then. Three hundred thousand francs. Take it or leave it –

OONA Goodbye Mr Kidnapper –

STEFAN Two hundred thousand...?

She hangs up. **STEFAN** *begins to vandalise the phone box.*

ALEK You can get in trouble for that Stefan...

STEFAN *vandalises it even more furiously.*

Scene Three

In a bar, Stefan is paralytic.

ALEK *sits beside him.*

In a room off-stage comes the muffled sound of music and clapping.

ALEK Did we...er...make a mistake kidnapping a dead person?

STEFAN It is a good plan.

ALEK Yea, I know, it's brilliant...just maybe we should've got someone who was alive? Or at least...a dead person who wasn't Buddhist.

STEFAN's *head starts sinking to the table.*

Just like that health insurance thing –

STEFAN That was a good plan.

ALEK I know. But that was the giveaway, wasn't it. When the police searched your house, and they found all these unpaid bills. You didn't have a hand, and the only bill you'd paid was the health insurance –

STEFAN You ever had any better ideas, Mr Einstein?

STEFAN *pulls out more money and gives it to* **ALEK.**

Beer.

His head falls onto the table.

ALEK Where did you get this money? Stefan?

STEFAN's *asleep.*

In the back room the music finishes, to loud roars and claps.

SYLVIE *emerges wearing traditional Swiss dress, breathing heavily.*

She heads for the bar, and stops dead.

SYLVIE Alek?

STEFAN *wakes, trying to focus.*

Stefan. What are you...?

STEFAN Sylvie?

SYLVIE Why aren't you at work?

STEFAN Because... I am drinking. What are you –?

SYLVIE They have sacked you!

STEFAN No, no. It is...a half-day. And what – why are you dancing your little dance?

SYLVIE You earn nothing. So I have to.

STEFAN Ah, but I do. Aha. *(He pulls out some notes)* See? Barman! A drink for my wife.

SYLVIE You have been paid?

STEFAN I have. Sit. Sit.

She sits.

SYLVIE And this is how you spend your wages? I save. You drink?

STEFAN No. No. No. No. My wages... I save. But this...this is extra. This is bonus. Because the boss is pleased with my pumping. I have a big bonus. Which is why we must celebrate!

He starts to fall asleep.

Champagne...!

He falls asleep.

ALEK *and* SYLVIE *exchange an awkward smile.*

SYLVIE Hello Alek.

ALEK Hi Sylvie.

SYLVIE It's been a long time. I miss your little visits.

ALEK Yes. But now you have Stefan, so...

SYLVIE I am glad he is doing so well at the garage.

ALEK You are looking very beautiful tonight.

SYLVIE You are sweet.

ALEK I hope you don't mind, and Stefan doesn't mind, but I think with every passing year you look more and more beautiful.

SYLVIE That is so lovely. Stefan never says anything like that –

ALEK I have not had sex for four years.

An awkward silence.

SYLVIE Stefan should get you work in his garage.

She nudges STEFAN *awake.*

Stefan, why can't you get Alek some work in the garage?

STEFAN What?

ALEK I'd like that. I'd like to work at your garage.

STEFAN What are you doing here?

SYLVIE Celebrating.

STEFAN Ah yes. My promotion!

SYLVIE I thought it was a bonus.

STEFAN Yes. It is. A bonus AND a promotion. I am now the man in charge of four pumps! An entire forecourt. That is worth celebrating. Yes? Barman! Champagne! No – *(he gets up suddenly)* better than that! Let us go... CLUBBING!

He falls into –

Scene Four

A club, with pumping seventies disco music.

STEFAN *is fast asleep on the dance floor.* ALEK *and* SYLVIE *dance awkwardly around him. They begin, gradually, to move a little easier to the music.*

The music changes to a slow ballad.

SYLVIE How is work? Stefan says you are busy fixing cars.

ALEK No. No, it's quiet at the moment. Lonely. How about you?

She gestures to her costume, as she dances.

SYLVIE Well, I am doing this. I am not good enough at sewing. Not yet.

ALEK You will have your haberdashery.

SYLVIE You remembered.

ALEK Of course I remembered. That's why I...

SYLVIE What?

They dance a little closer, almost touching.

Alek?

STEFAN *rises groggily from the floor.*

STEFAN What are we doing here?

SYLVIE Celebrating your success.

He starts to dance drunkenly with SYLVIE.

STEFAN Well, there's only one way to really celebrate my success.

He gropes her lecherously.

Make babies!

SYLVIE *extricates herself.*

SYLVIE Don't even presume to be capable.

SYLVIE *walks off.*

STEFAN *gives* **ALEK** *the thumbs up, and staggers after her.*

ALEK *walks into...*

Scene Five

The lock-up.

He stands alone for a moment.

He walks to the radio and turns it on.

NEWSRDR – have traced the phone-calls to the Lausanne area. Police are now focusing their search within that quiet, lakeside town –

ALEK *turns it off.*

Terrified, he walks into –

Scene Six

The countryside. A phone box.

He approaches STEFAN, *who's wearing a long coat and shades.*

They look round nervously, and dial.

OONA *answers wearily.*

OONA Hello?

STEFAN *(yelling)* I want one hundred thousand francs in a suitcase –

OONA Soon you'll be paying us to have him back –

STEFAN – in a suitcase, under the bench, by the lake. If it's not there by tomorrow morning –

OONA We won't get Charlie back.

STEFAN I'll shoot your grandchildren's legs off!

Pause.

OONA I'm sorry?

STEFAN You heard. Little Christopher's first. I'll track him down, and I'll shoot his bloody legs off. Right?

STEFAN *slams down the phone.*

ALEK You can't do that!

STEFAN Yes, I can. Everyone's at it. It is how the world works... whoever's got the biggest gun.

ALEK But you haven't got a gun.

STEFAN *pulls a shotgun from his coat.*

How have you –?

He gives the gun to ALEK.

STEFAN You know what you've got to do.

Blackout.

ACT V

Scene One

In the lock-up, ALEK *is putting tools away, and wiping oil from his hands.*

ALEK I'm scared, Charlie. You always knew how to get out of scrapes. Bopping that big bully with a brick – he swings, you duck – bop – he swings – you duck – bop and he's wobbling...and whack...he goes down. Brilliant. Then dust yourself down, click your heels, and do your funny walk down the road...

Suddenly a police siren sounds in the distance.

ALEK *freezes, as the siren gets closer and closer.*

Gradually, the sound fades away again.

It was the ringleaders they wanted. Mum – she was the first, you see. Stopped working...got all the women to walk out with her. Dad followed, and so did all the men.

ALEK *sits down, and picks up the gun. It's sawn off now, and mounted on a hand attachment. He polishes it.*

They took them away in a Moskvitch 423. I remember that because it's the same car they built in the factory. Moskvitch 402, 410, and the 423 station wagon.

He points the gun, squinting, checking the alignment.

It was a shit car. I kept thinking it was going to break down. But it didn't. And that was the last time I saw them...

There is a heavy knock on the door.

The knock comes again.

SYLVIE Alek? Alek? Are you in there?

ALEK Sylvie?

SYLVIE Can I come in?

ALEK How are things?

SYLVIE Alek, can you open up? There's something wrong with my 2CV.

ALEK You need to book her in.

SYLVIE Alek! It's me. What's the matter? Are we not friends any more? Oh, have you got a girl in there?

ALEK No.

SYLVIE You're allowed to. I'd be pleased if you had, after so long –

ALEK Yea, there's a girl in here.

SYLVIE Get rid of her. I need you, Alek. Now. I really, really need you.

ALEK Just a minute – *(loudly)* you've got to go. Bye-bye. Yes. Out the back.

He quickly tidies up, hides the gun, and covers up the coffin with a tarpaulin. He sprays air freshener around. He opens the door. **SYLVIE** *comes in, wearing a coat, and holding a bag.*

Hi.

SYLVIE Hello.

ALEK She went out the back.

SYLVIE *begins to sniff the air. He sprays the air freshener around her head.*

What seems to be the trouble?

SYLVIE Do you know what Stefan's done?

ALEK Which...thing?

SYLVIE He stole my money. Everything I saved. Did you know that?

ALEK I didn't know that. I'm sorry.

SYLVIE No. You wouldn't lie to me. Not like Stefan. Well... I have to get away, a long way away, and the brakes...well, they're not right. They're not...

ALEK Braking?

SYLVIE See, you're good. Can you check them?

ALEK But why –

SYLVIE I'm leaving Stefan. I'm going to Zurich. Home to Papa. To beg his forgiveness. To tell him he was right.

> **SYLVIE** *starts to cry.* **ALEK** *gives her a cloth from his overalls. She wipes her nose and eyes. The cloth smears oil on her face.* **ALEK** *gives her another cloth to wipe it off, but makes it worse. Soon her face is covered in oil.*

Papa's not right, of course. You're proof of that. You should leave too. He's bad for both of us.

ALEK I'm nothing without Stefan.

SYLVIE No, he's nothing without you! We are the same, you and I. We make him what he is. He's a monster. Oh Alek, I dreamt of you last night.

ALEK Really? I dreamt of you too!

SYLVIE In mine you were torn. And moth-eaten. You'd been stuffed like a pigeon! But you had a big hole here, and inside there was a screaming wind and black emptiness...

ALEK I dreamt we had some spaghetti. It was nice.

> *Silence.*

I'll do those brakes –

SYLVIE I wanted to give you this, before I go.

She pulls the teddy bear attachment out of her bag.

It's yours isn't it. You made it for me.

ALEK How did you know?

SYLVIE It's always you. It's very soft...and very kind.

ALEK He was a birthday present.

SYLVIE They must have loved you very much.

Beat.

And the sewing machine. That was you as well. Do you remember the day we met, on the road to Lausanne?

ALEK How could I forget?

SYLVIE I don't remember you at all. That's the thing. All I saw was Stefan.

ALEK I mended your car.

SYLVIE I know. I was blind. I can see now.

She moves closer.

And you have lied about one thing.

ALEK Have I?

SYLVIE There was no girl in here.

ALEK No.

SYLVIE There is now.

She kisses him.

ALEK You mean you?

SYLVIE Yes.

Scene Two

ALEK *and* SYLVIE *lie sprawled, post-coital.*

SYLVIE Alek, for a man who has not had sex for four years –

ALEK Ever.

SYLVIE Ever?

ALEK Ever.

SYLVIE That was very good. How do you know what to do?

ALEK I just approached you like I would an old car.

SYLVIE Well. You are a very fine mechanic.

There is a heavy knocking at the door. She freezes.

STEFAN *(offstage, urgent)* Open it. Alek. It's me.

ALEK *gets up, horrified.* SYLVIE *stares.*

Get this door open.

ALEK You need to hide.

STEFAN It's crawling with cops out here. *(Yelling)* Get this door open.

SYLVIE *runs to the tarpaulin covering the coffin –*

ALEK No, not –

SYLVIE *hides under it with the coffin.*

ALEK *lets* STEFAN *in.*

STEFAN We need to bury him until we finish this. Have you done it?

ALEK What?

STEFAN The gun?

ALEK Yea.

ALEK *gets out the gun attachment.* STEFAN *grabs it.*

Careful –

SYLVIE *gags. The tarpaulin rises like an apparition, and she appears from under it. They all stare at each other, and the coffin.*

SYLVIE What is...why is there a...why have you got a...?

STEFAN What the hell is she doing here?

ALEK She wanted me to fix her car and –

SYLVIE Oh my God...tell me this isn't...

STEFAN It isn't. She was lying. She wanted to snoop –

SYLVIE Tell me this isn't Charlie Chaplin.

STEFAN It's not Charlie Chaplin.

STEFAN *realises that she's not wearing her dress.* ALEK *does up his flies.*

What are you –?

SYLVIE Is this Charlie Chaplin?!

STEFAN Yes, it's Charlie Chaplin!

SYLVIE No, no. Oh no. It can't be...

STEFAN What have you two been –?

SYLVIE You're the... Oh my God. You're the –?

STEFAN Alek?

SYLVIE This is your job isn't it?

ALEK I'm sorry –

SYVLIE This is the garage. This is our future.

STEFAN What have you been doing with my wife?

SYLVIE This is our cottage. And the garden. And the haberdashery.

STEFAN *(yelling)* Yes!

SYLVIE The body of Charlie Chaplin?

STEFAN It's a bloody good plan!

SYLVIE It's the worst plan you've ever had!

STEFAN The worst plan I ever had was marrying you! That you could do this...with my best friend? It's disgusting!

SYLVIE No. THIS is disgusting!

STEFAN Is this how you repay me?

SYLVIE Alek? How could you...?

She turns to go.

STEFAN Where are you going?

SYLVIE The police.

STEFAN I'll go to prison.

SYLVIE I want you in prison. You've lied to me too many times.

STEFAN You lied first!

SYLVIE When?

STEFAN The day we got married! You knew they weren't coming. But you never said a thing.

SYLVIE I didn't want to spoil your day.

STEFAN Yea? Well, you were not the woman I thought you were! If we'd had their money, none of this would've happened.

A police siren passes in the distance.

STEFAN *raises his hand, the gun attached to it.*

SYLVIE What is *that*?

STEFAN It's a sawn-off hand gun. Alek made it.

SYLVIE Alek?

STEFAN He does anything I ask him to.

STEFAN *points it at* **SYLVIE**.

SYLVIE You stole my money for this?

STEFAN Not stole. Invested. You put in, you get out.

SYLVIE You sound like Papa.

STEFAN Yea, well, this would've sealed the deal. Got us the money. We'd have had our dreams.

SYLVIE My dreams are dead.

STEFAN Tie her up, Igor. Put her in the van with Charlie. We drive to the countryside, and dig a big hole.

ALEK Don't make me –

STEFAN *points the gun right at* **SYLVIE**'*s head*.

SYLVIE You'd really shoot me?

STEFAN Yea. It's the way the world works. If you want to win, someone will lose.

SYLVIE Oh my God! I have married my father!

STEFAN Do it! You were nothing when we came here. I made you. I gave you life. Tie her up.

ALEK *gets some rope and starts tying her up*.

SYLVIE Alek? Don't. Is this what your parents taught you? Don't – stop, please –

STEFAN *puts a strip of gaffer tape over her mouth*.

STEFAN Right.

SYLVIE *is furiously trying to say something behind her gag*.

What? What's she saying?

SYLVIE *says it again*.

ALEK I think she's saying something about "the brakes".

STEFAN Yea, she's lying again. There's nothing wrong with the brakes.

Blackout.

Scene Three

A shadow play:

The 2CV, with a coffin sticking out of the back, drives out of the town, and up and down hills. A cow appears in front of them. The car can't stop.

Blackout.

We hear yells and screams, and finally, an enormous crash that goes on for an age.

Silence.

Scene Four

Lights rise on a scene of devastation.

The car is smashed up. **STEFAN** *and* **SYLVIE** *lie motionless. The coffin hangs out of the back. The cardboard cutout cow stands to one side. It moos.*

ALEK *rises and staggers from the wreckage, blood on his brow.*

He goes to the front of the car, and repeatedly tries to jump-start the car.

On the third attempt, something stirs in the wreck.

We hear a simple piano melody.

A hand comes out of the coffin, a cane, then a bowler hat.

Finally **CHARLIE CHAPLIN**'s *little tramp clambers out. He tries to walk, dizzy, like he's received a blow to the head.*

ALEK Charlie?

The tramp steadies himself, puts on his bowler hat, and positions his cane.

Charlie is that really you?

The tramp smiles, and flicks his hat in the air. **ALEK** *laughs.*

Oh, Charlie, I'm so glad you're alive.

He starts walking around, swinging his cane. He does a pratfall.

ALEK *laughs.*

It's like old times. Do you remember, Charlie? Row G. Mum and Dad...you on the big screen.

The tramp gets up and brushes himself down.

If only you could talk, Charlie.

The tramp gestures silently; on the screen we see silent film-style captions.

Caption: "I can talk".

Of course you can, sorry.

A voice emerges, strange and ethereal, but somehow **CHAPLIN.**

CHAPLIN I did the talkies, you know.

ALEK *is stunned.*

ALEK I... I only saw the early stuff.

The tramp shrugs, accepting this. He waddles off.

Sorry about digging you up, and everything.

The tramp starts examining the wreckage.

I can't believe you're here! Have I said...how much Mum and Dad loved you? Every time you were on...we were there.

CHAPLIN I gave them hope.

ALEK Yes...yes.

The tramp produces a flower from his pocket, and holds it aloft with a flourish.

You did.

The tramp finds the sawn-off handgun, and rather accusingly shows it to **ALEK.**

I know, um, Stefan wanted me to, so –

CHAPLIN Do you always do what bullies tell you?

ALEK What else can I do?

The tramp walks back and hands him the gun.

CHAPLIN You take him too seriously.

He starts walking back to the coffin.

I always found the bullies and tyrants of this world to be hilarious.

He climbs into the coffin.

There is only one thing to do when face to face with an idiot.

The tramp vanishes. The music cuts.

ALEK Charlie? Charlie?

ALEK *slowly becomes aware of* **STEFAN** *staggering from the wreckage, covered in blood, spade in hand, like a monster that refuses to die.*

STEFAN *(gasping)* This can still work.

SYLVIE *is also crawling from the wreckage, bruised and bloodied.*

We find Charlie. Go for the boy. Shoot his legs off. Get the cash. Catch a train. Head for the border.

STEFAN *thrusts the spade at* **ALEK**.

Dig. Go on. Dig a big hole.

ALEK No.

STEFAN What?

ALEK *slowly raises the gun until it is pointing at* **STEFAN**.

ALEK No.

STEFAN Hang on, hang on –?

ALEK Run, Sylvie.

SYLVIE *gets to her feet.*

STEFAN What? You think she's worth this? Just because she –

SYLVIE *staggers up to* STEFAN *and slaps him round the face.*

ALEK Run!

SYLVIE *starts to run, but can't help herself; she goes back and kicks* STEFAN *in the bollocks. He doubles up and falls over, groaning.*

(Yelling) Run...!

Again she is about to go, but runs back and kicks ALEK *in the balls.*

SYLVIE *exits.*

For a while they both lie both groaning on the floor, incapable of anything.

STEFAN She'll get the –

STEFAN *struggles to the gun, screws it on as fast as he can, and shoots uselessly into the distance.*

You idiot. That's it. That is it.

STEFAN *raises the gun.*

I should've done this years ago, the day we met.

He points it at ALEK*'s head.*

I should've put you down.

ALEK *starts to smile, and can't help a giggle.*

What?

ALEK *giggles more.*

ALEK That's it.

STEFAN What's so funny?

ALEK You are.

STEFAN No, I'm not.

> *He guffaws loudly, unable to stop himself.*

I'm about to blow your head off. That funny, is it?

ALEK Yes! Do it! Because I'm not scared any more. Whatever you do...it'll be hilarious.

STEFAN Are you laughing at me!

ALEK What else is there to do? You're an idiot. I should have done this years ago.

STEFAN Stop laughing!

ALEK That's what's special about Charlie! He makes me strong!

STEFAN *(pressing the gun to* ALEK's *head)* I've got the gun. You've got nothing. So who's strong now?

> STEFAN *presses the trigger.*
>
> *A flower pops out of the barrel.*
>
> *There is a moment's silence.*
>
> STEFAN *looks directly down the barrel.*

Did you do this?

ALEK Charlie did it.

STEFAN Shut up about Charlie Chaplin!

ALEK Do you know what's really special about him?

> STEFAN *presses the trigger repeatedly.*

He never, ever dies!

> STEFAN *lets out a yell. He falls to the ground. He begins to cry.*

In the distance, we hear police sirens.

STEFAN *(weakly)* I can't go to prison.

ALEK *waves and shouts.*

ALEK We're over here!

STEFAN *stands, and desperately points the flower gun towards the approaching police.*

STEFAN I'm not going to prison!

They are surrounded by flashing blue light, and blaring sirens.

ALEK It's alright! We've got Charlie! He's OK.

We hear a megaphone from off.

POLICE You are surrounded! Put down your weapon!

ALEK Put it down, Stefan.

STEFAN This can still work.

POLICE Put down your weapon.

STEFAN This can still work –!

With the sound of a gunshot –

– we cut to black.

Scene Five

ALEK *and* STEFAN *are stood side by side in the dock, their hands cuffed.* STEFAN's *head is bandaged.*

We hear the voice of a JUDGE.

JUDGE Stefan Shopivich Debylanov, on the charges of disturbing the dead, and extortion, do you plead guilty or not guilty?

STEFAN Not guilty.

JUDGE Aleksander Leopold, on the charges of disturbing the dead, and extortion, do you plead guilty or not guilty?

ALEK Guilty. Very guilty.

STEFAN *stares at him with contempt.*

I also kept him in the lock-up...for ages. Which wasn't very nice for him, so...

JUDGE The defendant may sit.

ALEK Also it was me who chopped Stefan's hand off. So I'm accessory to fraud...er... and I slept with his wife. Actually I'm quite proud of that.

JUDGE Have you finished?

ALEK Yep.

EPILOGUE

Mist rises. Bolts slide. Enormous iron gates open.

ALEK *emerges onto the street, dishevelled, with a small case.*

The gates clang shut.

He looks around him. He's completely alone.

He sits on his case. He wonders what to do.

He turns to the audience.

ALEK In 1978 two Eastern European, refugee, auto-mechanics kidnapped and ransomed the body of Charlie Chaplin, because they wanted money to set up their very own garage. The ringleader got four and a half years hard labour. His accomplice got hardly anything at all. Charlie got eternity... re-buried under six feet of concrete.

ALEK *gets up, and dusts himself down.*

Just as he's about to turn away and walk off, **SYLVIE** *appears through the mist, dressed in smart clothes, and carrying a small case.*

He stares. She stares back. She smiles.

They walk towards each other. They kiss.

They walk off down the open road.

Caption: The End

PROPERTY LIST

Toolbox (p2)
Axe (p3)
There is an old mattress on the floor with a teddy bear on it
There are tools, an old radio, some tins and the odd tyre (p8)
Beer (p8)
Bottle opener (p8)
Envelope (p11)
Needle and thread (p12)
Carrots. A rabbit. Some rocks. Soup (p12)
A small stuffed squirrel (p14)
Bundle of cloth (p17)
A large spanner attachment (p17)
An old sewing machine (p17)
A very large, very heavy coffin (p21)
Sewing machine (p24)
Sylvie is sewing the eyes on a stuffed animal (p25)
Other dead creatures surround her, waiting to be mended (p25)
Sewing machine (p25)
Coins (p27)
Money (p29)
Money box (p33)
Large wad of notes (p34)
Two notes (p34)
A "pair of pliers" hand attachment (p35)
Teddy bear (p36)
Wrench (p37)
Polaroid camera (p37)
Piece of metal (p40)
Teddy bear (p40)
Axe (p42)
...pulls aside the coffin lid, and pulls out an arm (p42)
Envelope (p43)
More money (p46)
Shotgun (p52)
Alek – putting tools away and wiping oil from his hands (p54)
Gun – it's sawn off now, and mounted on a hand attachment
(p54)
Covers the coffin with a tarpaulin (p55)
Sprays air freshener around (p55)

Cloth (p56)
The cloth smears oil on her face. Alek gives her another cloth to wipe it off... Soon her face is covered in oil (p56)
Teddy bear attachment (p57)
Rope (p61)
Strip of gaffer tape (p61)
Flower (p65)
Sawn-off handgun (p65)
Spade (p66)
Stefan presses the trigger. A flower pops out of the barrel (p68)

Costume:

Two shabby men appear, wearing long coats and carrying battered suitcases (p1)
Sylvie – dressed in traditional Swiss costume (p1)
Stefan – unbuttons his shirt to reveal a forest of chest hair (p2)
Stefan – long coat with a very long prisoner's beard (p5)
Stefan slowly removes his hand from his pocket. There is a large, gruesome hook on the end of it (p5)
Sylvie – a plain dress (p12)
Alek and Stefan rub mud on their faces. They put balaclavas over their heads. Stefan screws a spade attachment onto his arm (p21)
Alek & Stefan – covered in mud (p22)
Stefan – coat (p23)
Stefan is now smarter, and beardless (p29)
Alek – a child's outfit round his neck (p35)
Oona Chaplin – appears dressed in black (p38)
Stefan – Swiss hat and coat (p41)
Sylvie – traditional Swiss dress (p41)
Alek – joins in with his tools (p41)
Sylvie – traditional Swiss dress (p47)
Stefan – long coat and shades (p52)
Sylvie – wearing a coat and holding a bag (p55)
Stefan's head is bandaged (p70)
Alek – dishevelled, with a small case (p71)
Sylvie – dressed in smart clothes, and carrying a small case (p71)

LIGHTING

Lights up (p1)
Blackout (p2)
Blackout (p15)
Blackout (p29)
A flick of light...light flickers on his face (p35)
Blackout (p39)
Blackout (p53)
Blackout (p62)
Blackout (p63)
Lights rise on a scene of devastation (p64)
Surrounded by flashing blue light (p69)
We cut to black (p69)

SOUND/EFFECTS

A caption card, like that from a silent film, is projected onto a screen:
Caption: Switzerland. Land of Opportunity (p1)
The cow moos. Birds sing (p1)
We hear loud Swiss folk music (p1)
Caption: Opportunity Number One (p1)
Suddenly the car stops, and the music cuts. The engine makes an exploding sound, and a puff of dirty smoke comes out of the bonnet (p2)
Caption: Opportunity Number Two (p3)
Blood starts spurting from the wound (p4)
Blood pumping from his stump (p4)
Mist rises. Bolts slide. Enormous iron gates open (p5)
The gates slam shut behind him (p5)
Loud seventies disco music (p16)
The music cuts and the engine bursts into life (p16)
Engine dies (p17)
The engine springs to life (p20)
A caption reads: Opportunity Number Three (p21)
Stefan turns on the radio (p22)
Stefan delightedly turns down the radio (p22)
Radio (p31)
Stefan irritably snaps off the radio (p31)
The click-click of a projector (p35)

A phone is ringing on a table (p38)
We begin to hear Swiss folk music (p41)
On the screen we see images of picture book Switzerland: mountains and lakes, skiing and alpine horns (p41)
On the screen behind we see images of wealth: yachts, bankers and money (p41)
Music (p43)
Stefan and Alek saw off various parts of Chaplin's corpse, body parts wing their way through the air (p43)
The music cuts (p43)
The muffled sound of music and clapping (p46)
In the backroom the music finishes, to loud roars and claps (p46)
A club, with pumping seventies disco music (p49)
The music changes to a slow ballad (p49)
Alek walks to the radio and turns it on (p51)
Alek turns it off (p51)
Suddenly a police siren sounds in the distance (p54)
The siren gets closer and closer (p54)
The sound fades away again (p54)
There is a heavy knock on the door (p55)
The knock comes again (p55)
Heavy knocking at the door (p58)
A police siren passes in the distance (p60)
A shadow play: The 2CV, with a coffin sticking out of the back, drives out of the town, and up and down hills. A cow appears in front of them. The car can't stop. Blackout. We hear yells and screams, and finally, an enormous crash that goes on for an age. Silence (p63)
Cow – moos (p64)
Alek – blood on his brow (p64)
Repeatedly tries to jump-start the car (p64)
On the third attempt, something stirs in the wreck (p64)
We hear a simple piano melody (p64)
The music cuts (p66)
Stefan – covered in blood (p66)
Sylvie – bruised and bloodied (p66)
In the distance we hear police sirens (p69)
Surrounded...blaring sirens (p69)
We hear a megaphone from off (p69)
With the sound of a gunshot (p69)

Mist rises. Bolts slide. Enormous iron gates open (p71)
The gates clang shut (p71)
Caption: The End (p71)

THIS
IS
NOT
THE
END

Lightning Source UK Ltd.
Milton Keynes UK
UKHW021627260220
359368UK00006BA/427

9 780573 113994